R64049.

KW-052-255

WITHDRAWN

© Aladdin Books Ltd 2001

Designed and produced by
Aladdin Books Ltd
28 Percy Street
London W1P 0LD

First published in
Great Britain in 2001 by
Franklin Watts
96 Leonard Street
London EC2A 4XD

ISBN 0 7496 4118 5
A catalogue record for this
book is available from the
British Library.

Printed in Belgium

All rights reserved

Editor
Bibby Whittaker

Literacy Consultant
Ann Hawken,
Westminster Institute of Education,
Oxford Brookes University

Design
Flick, Book Design and Graphics

Picture Research
Brian Hunter Smart

READING ABOUT

My Family

By Jim Pipe

EDUCATION RESOURCE SERVICE
GLASGOW

Aladdin/Watts
London • Sydney

Family pictures

2

Hi! I am Anthony.

I am making a family tree. This shows everyone in my family.

Would you like to meet them?

Making a family tree

This is my mother.

Her name is Angela, but I call her Mum. Here she is making a cake.

Making a cake

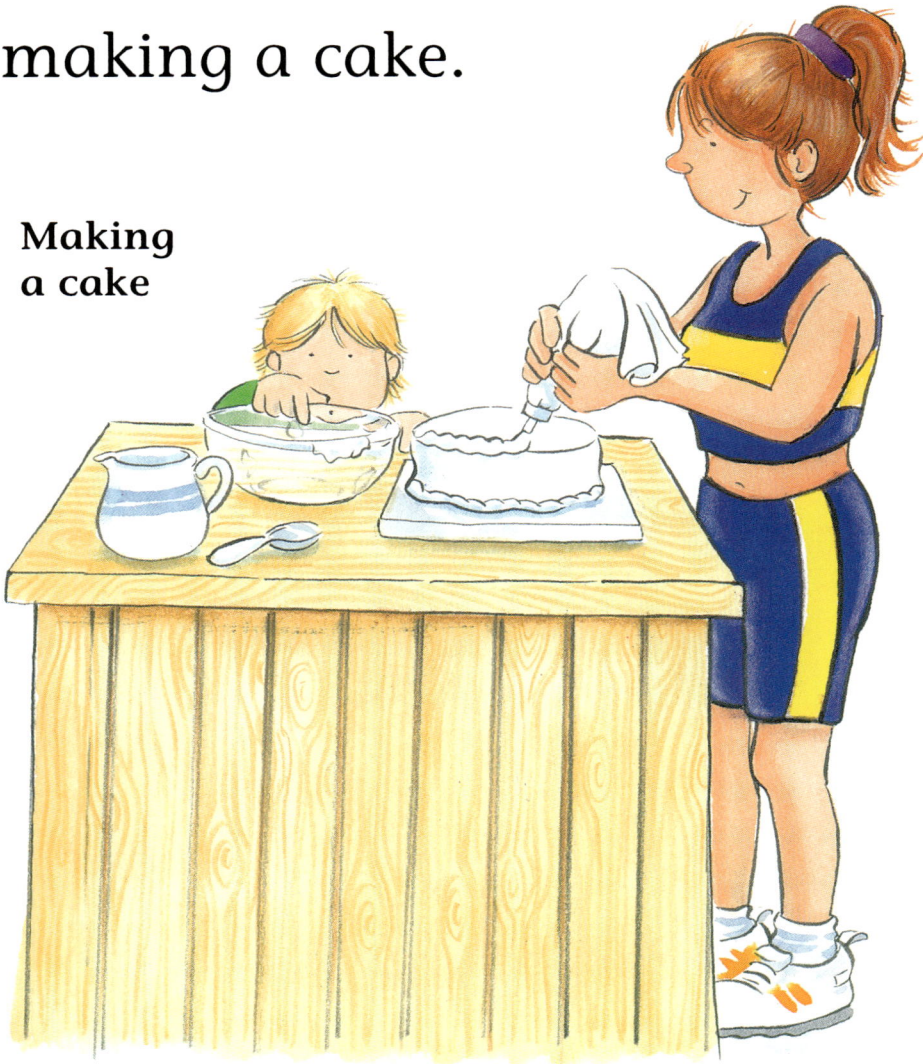

Mum used to be a dancer.

Now she runs classes at the gym.

At the gym

This is my father.

His name is Roger, but most people call him Spike. I call him Dad.

He drives a big digger and helps to build the roads.

Dad

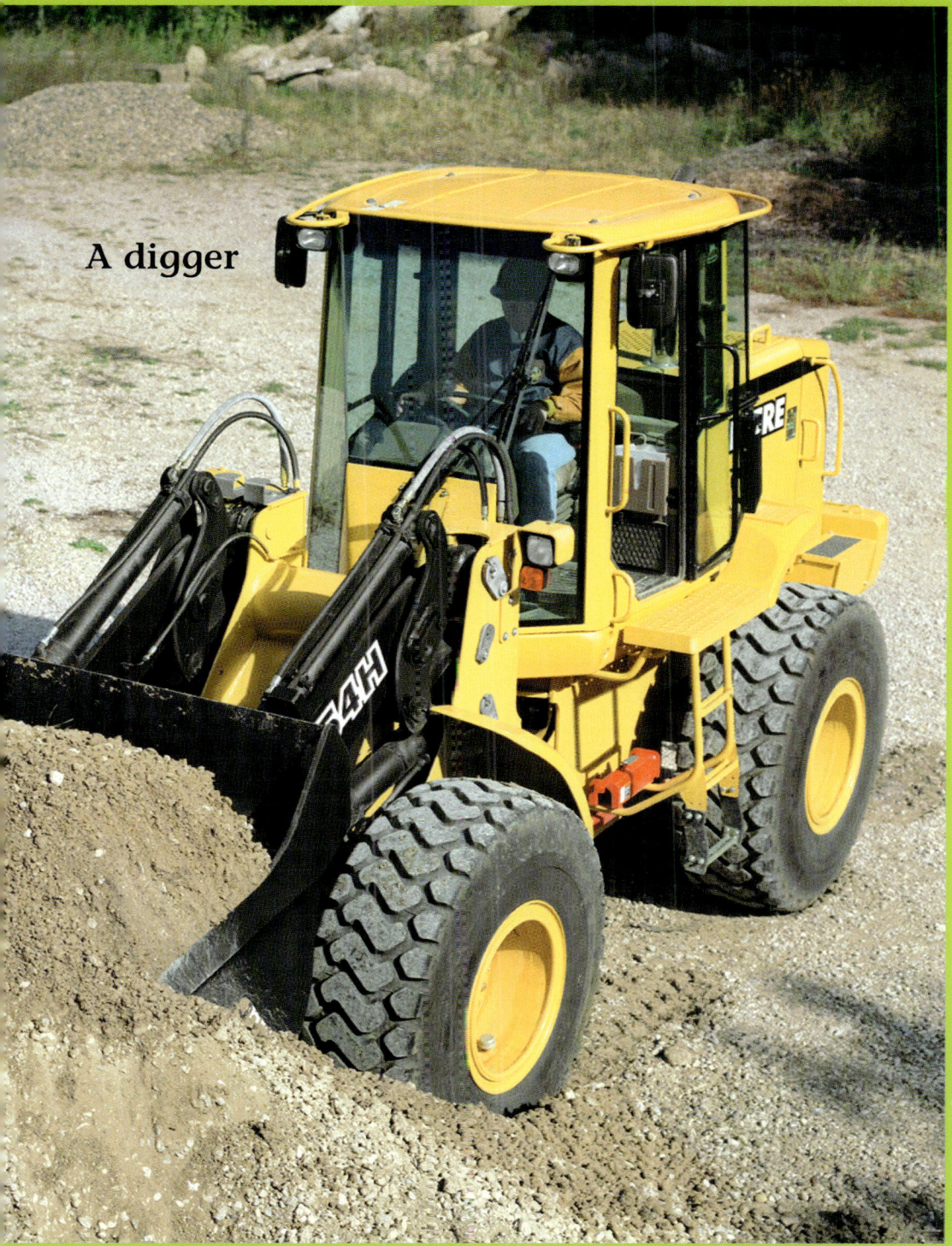

A digger

Meet my sister Karen.

She is twelve and plays the flute
in the school band.

School band

Sometimes she helps me with my homework.

Doing my homework

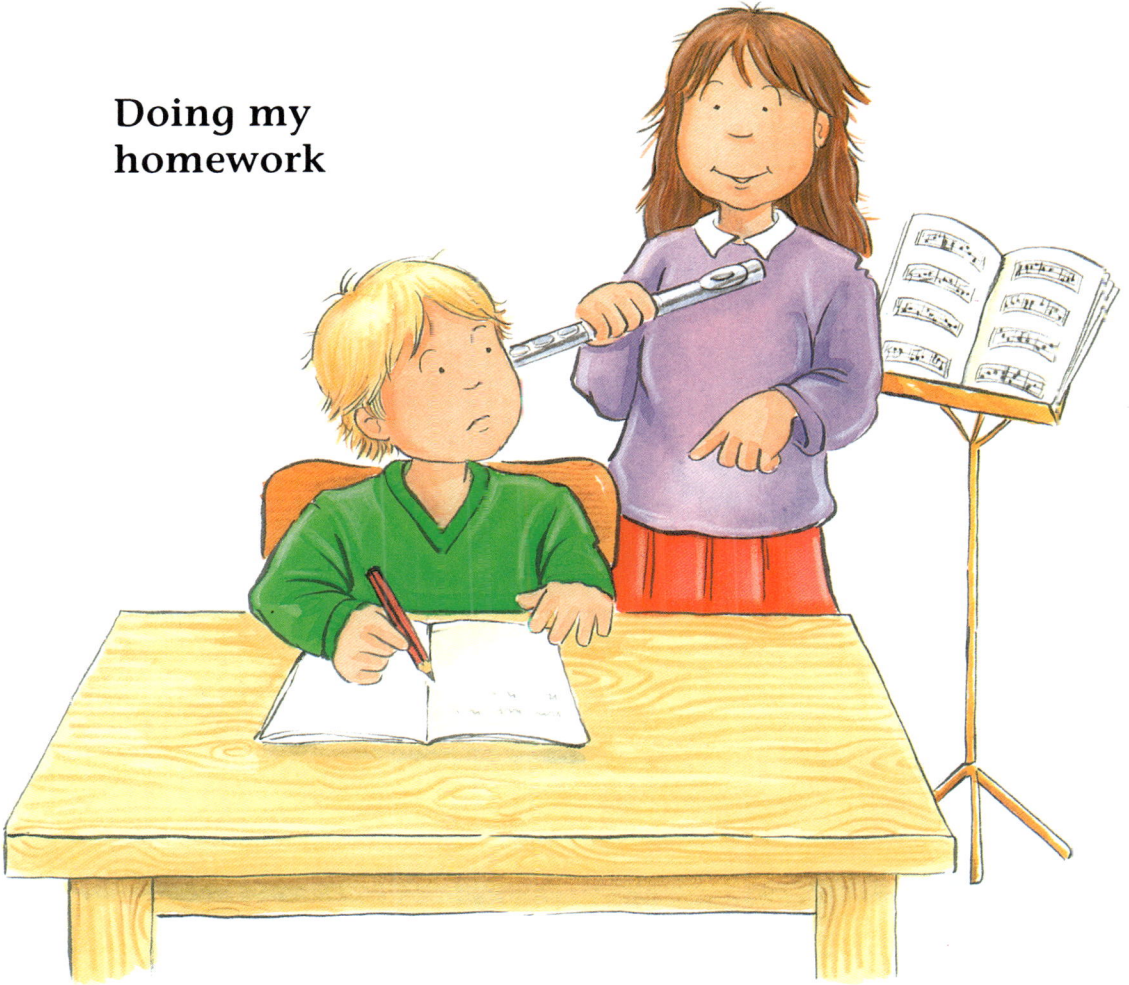

But sometimes my sister can be very bossy.

This is my baby brother Tim.

He is only three.

He is still learning to talk,
so he calls me "Ant".

Baby
brother

I like playing with him sometimes.

But when my friends are here,
I want him to go away.

Playing
with friends

I have four grandparents.
Here are Dad's mum and dad.

When I visit them, Grandpa
takes me fishing.
Grandma
likes to go
swimming.

Grandparents

Fishing

Uncle Frank is Mum's brother.

He drives a fast red car and likes to honk its horn.

Mum says he is very silly.

Fast car

But when Uncle Frank makes silly faces, we all laugh.

He can also do great magic tricks.

Doing a magic trick

Uncle Matt is my Dad's brother.

He is a fire fighter. He wears a special suit with a yellow helmet.

Fire fighter

Aunt Marie is his wife. Their baby is called Ricky.

Ricky is my cousin. He does not do much, but he makes lots of noise.

My uncle

My cousin and I

My aunt

Guess what!

Today is my birthday and everyone has come for my party.

Look at all my presents!

Presents

Can you guess which present
Uncle Matt gave me?

Here is my family tree.

All my grandparents
are at the top.

My parents, aunt and
uncles are in the middle.

At the bottom are my
cousin, my brother,
my sister...

...and ME, Anthony!

Family tree

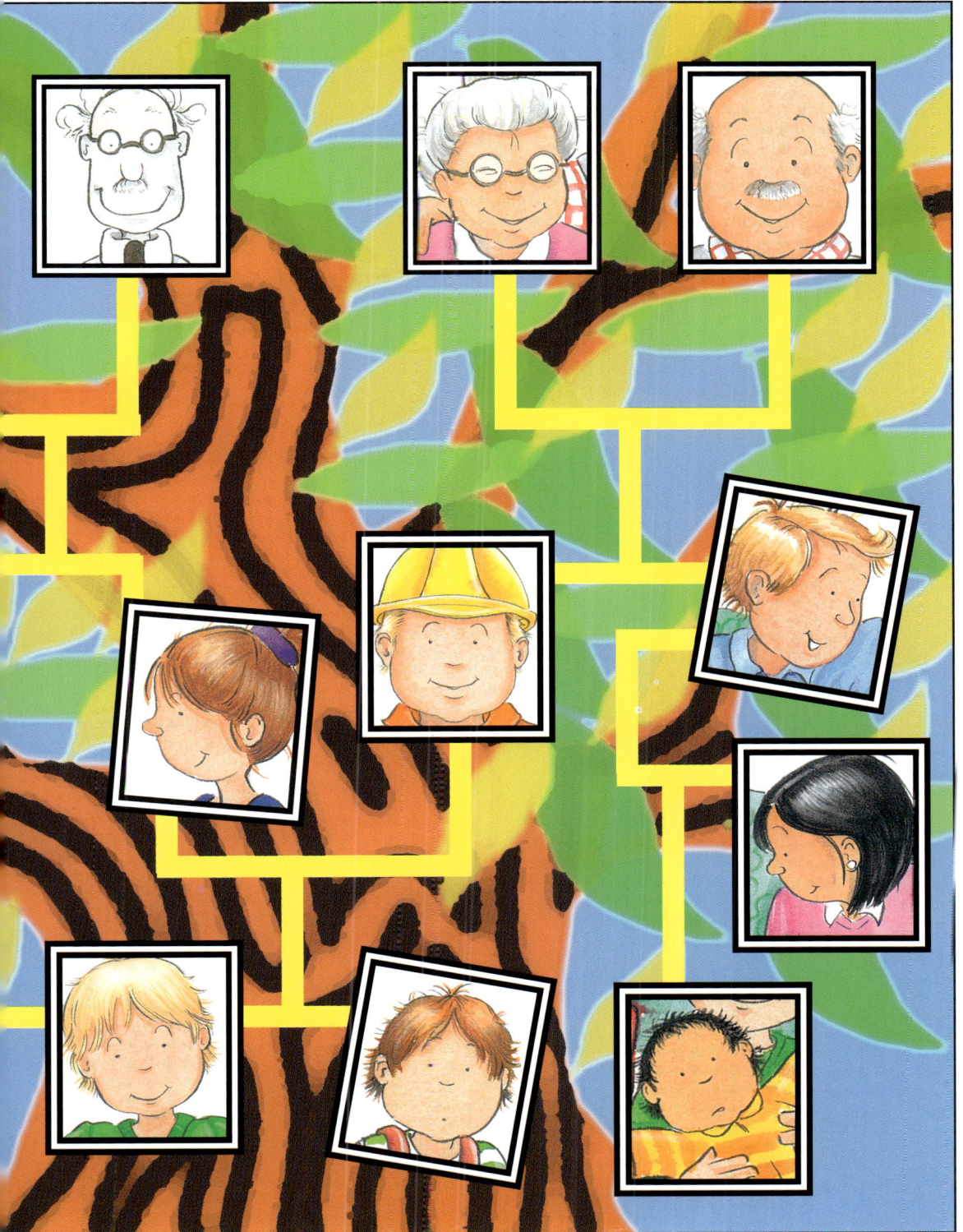

Here are some words and phrases from the book.

Grandparents

Make a family tree

Drive a car

Cousin

Aunt and uncle

At the gym

Play with friends

Sister

Go fishing

Do homework

Can you use these words to write your own story?

Did you see these in the book?

Lamp

Teddy bear

Hose

Saxophone

Illustrator: Mary Lonsdale for SGA
Picture Credits:
Abbreviations: t – top, m – middle, b – bottom, r – right, l – left, c – centre. Cover, 2, 14, 18-19, 22, 24tl, 24tr – Select Pictures; 5, 23tr – Steve Chenn/CORBIS; 7 – John Deere; 8, 24br – Bob Rowan: Progressive Image/CORBIS; 13, 23ml – Bob Winsett/CORBIS; 16, 24bl – Scania.